The Zero Hour Workweek

The Zero Hour Workweek

*How I Liberated Myself from the 9 to 5
by Getting Paid to Be Me*

Jonathan Mead

WAKING LION PRESS

ISBN 978-1-4341-0320-8

The views expressed in this book are the responsibility of the author and do not necessarily represent the position of the publisher. The reader alone is responsible for the use of any ideas or information provided by this book.

Published by Waking Lion Press, an imprint of The Editorium

Any additions to original text (publisher's preface, editor's notes, etc.) © 2011 by The Editorium. All rights reserved. Printed in the United States of America.

Waking Lion Press™, the Waking Lion Press logo, and The Editorium™ are trademarks of The Editorium, LLC

The Editorium, LLC
West Valley City, UT 84128-3917
wakinglionpress.com
wakinglion@editorium.com

Contents

Introduction: What Is This All About? vii

1 My Story 1

2 My Journey to Getting Paid to Be Me 7

3 Zero-Hour Case Studies 29

4 Your Paid-to-Exist Secret Weapon 40

5 The World Needs You to Do What You Love 52

What's Next? 55

Share 56

Acknowledgments 57

Introduction: What Is This All About?

Is it possible to get paid to exist? To live in a way where you can't tell the difference between when you're working and when you're playing?

For a long time, I searched for the answer to this question. And as I searched, it didn't seem many people were on my side. Some people believed it was possible to do what you love, but that meant you had to be broke or a starving artist. Some believed that it was a life reserved for the rich minority. And some believed it was only possible for people born with natural genius or prodigal talent.

But most people just believed it was silly. You're just supposed to accept that work is something you *have to do* and that you *don't like.*

Well, I found out something interesting. Just because most people believed that work was meant to be a chore, didn't make it a fact.

It was really an agreement.

So I decided to stop agreeing, and see what happened.

What I found is that most of our ideas of what

we think to be true are really *assumptions.* If you test those assumptions, you'll probably find out something even more interesting. You can *choose* to design your life in whatever way you see fit. *You* make the agreement.

In other words, yes, it is possible to get paid to exist. Yes, it is possible to get paid to be who you are. I know it is, because I've done it.

But what is "getting paid to exist?" What does that even mean?

Do I mean getting paid to just be alive? To sit on a couch all day and watch reruns of *Seinfeld?* Or to lay on a beach, drinking martinis while rubbing cocoa butter all over your body? No, that's not what I mean. And honestly, while that might be fun for a couple of weeks, you'd probably get bored with that after a while.

You'd probably want something more. You'd probably want to make a difference and give other people some kind of value. And you would want to do it in a way that makes you come alive, makes you excited, and allows you to do the things you're *naturally* good at.

That is what "getting paid to exist" is all about. It's about getting paid to be who you are by leveraging your unique strengths, doing what you love, and finding a way to channel that so you can provide value to others while you're doing it.

I found out a way to do this for myself, only after

I tested my assumptions about what I thought was possible and what was not.

But it wasn't easy.

See, I knew that this is what I wanted, but I didn't think it was possible. I grew up with the idea that work was supposed to be a grim duty of paying your dues and "sucking it up."

It turns out, not only was that complete bullshit, but living your life like that is actually a slap in the face to life itself.

If there is any purpose to life, isn't it to enjoy it? Isn't that the ultimate goal of everything you do?

So, wouldn't it make much more sense to bypass suffering now ("work") for happiness later ("living")? Wouldn't it be much nicer if we could just *eliminate* the problem of "work/life balance?" Wouldn't it be nice if you couldn't tell the difference between when you're "working" and when you're "playing?"

I personally can no longer tell the difference.

I don't feel a difference between my work on the one hand and "the rest of my life" on the other. I don't count down the time to five o'clock. I don't dread Mondays and I never feel that my weekend was too short.

If this sounds interesting to you, I'd like to show you how I created a life where I "get paid to be me." I'll bring you behind the scenes, tell you my personal story, and give you a blueprint for how you can do the same in your life.

Your journey will obviously be a little different than mine. That's OK. While I think modeling others and mentorship is a way to fast-track success, I know that it's equally important to live on your own terms. That's the whole point of getting paid to exist, anyway. *It's your game.* You design it and you decide how it's played.

With that in mind, getting paid to exist is just as much of an art as it is a science. So we're going to take a look at what this "working while playing" looks like. I feel that it's best described by Mr. Michener:

> *The master in the art of living*
> *draws no sharp distinction between*
> *his labor and his leisure,*
> *his mind and his body,*
> *his work and his play,*
> *his education and his recreation.*
> *He hardly knows which.*
> *He simply pursues his vision of excellence*
> *through whatever he is doing*
> *and leaves others to determine*
> *whether his is working or playing.*
> *To himself, he is always doing both.*
> —James A. Michener

But first, I'd like to tell you my story.

Part 1

My Story

Throughout my life, I've always had an issue with doing things based on someone else's idea of how I should do them. I've never been one to like rules, authority, and conventions that are not meant to be questioned.

I grew up in a very fundamentalist home in rural Idaho, and my parents were very conservative. We went to church on Sundays in the family station wagon. I went to public schools, and had a typical childhood. I tried to follow the rules and live the way I was told.

As I was growing up, I often didn't understand a lot of what the grown-ups taught. I didn't get it, so I would ask them about it. I wanted to know why. But most of the time they didn't have an answer. They would say "that's the way it is" or "because it's made that way."

Somewhere in me I realized that that was false. It didn't satisfy my curiosity. So I would ask "Why is it that way?" and I'd keep asking why when their answers didn't satisfy me. This eventually led to the adult becoming frustrated and telling me that I was too quizzical. I was left with a guilty feeling that something was wrong with me for being so curious. I didn't accept things the way everyone else did.

I felt like I didn't "get it." Maybe when I was older I'd understand. Maybe I wasn't smart enough.

But I still wondered.

I wondered why my parents hated their jobs. I wondered why people followed rules that didn't make sense. I wondered why the schools wouldn't let me learn what I wanted to learn.

I wondered lots of things. But more than anything, I wondered why people had to become "responsible."

Domestication and Responsibility

It seems there's a certain point, somewhere around the age eighteen to twenty, that people need to start "being responsible." It's not about fun anymore, it's about *being responsible.* In other words, it's time to stop having fun and start being serious. It's time to get a job and stop screwing around.

I never understood that. Why couldn't work be fun? Why did the work you have to do to survive have to make you unhappy? Wouldn't it be easier to just not participate in that?

For a long time I didn't know it was possible to stop

participating. I didn't realize that I could choose that, or something different.

That was until I started testing this convention: the cultural consensus that work *must not be fun.*

I don't care where you're born or what kind of upbringing you've had. All of us, on some level or another, have been influenced by this mammoth collective assumption. Despite our pre-domesticated inner conviction that work is meant to be sacred, we can't help but be subdued when pushed up against this social vortex.

Not only can we not help but be sucked in, we can't help but feel guilty for our desire to want to experience work that is meaningful, fulfilling, and a joy to engage in.

That feeling of guilt never sat well with me; something about it smelled fake. But years of domestication is hard to break.

Mind-Renting, Here I Come

So after I was lovingly kicked out by my mother's boyfriend at the tender age of sixteen, I began faithfully fulfilling my duty of "paying my dues." I first rented myself out to fast-food chains and data entry sweatshops.

Then I moved up in the world and got a job as a file clerk (or file hell liaison, a description I found much more precise). After a couple of years of mind-blowing excitement handling construction contract files, I finally got a job I was "supposed to like." I found a job in a multimedia department, managing an employee recognition program.

I have to admit, this was not a bad job. Managing a program where coworkers are recognizing each other for the great work they do is not a bad thing to wake up to. I was constantly surrounded by positive feedback, as someone whose job was to spread the word about the great work people do. I imagine I had it good compared to some other HR and PR positions that dealt with constantly putting out fires.

Even though sometimes I really enjoyed this job, *I knew I was still renting out my mind.* I was still letting someone else dictate how my energy was channeled. Someone else held the remote.

Now, you might argue that getting a check every two weeks warrants letting someone else control that remote. But I always felt that there was a better choice out there.

Notice that keyword there . . . *choice.*

You can choose to rent out your mind, or you can find a way to reclaim ownership of it.

So, the question is: How can we afford to buy back our own time? How can we pay ourselves to exist so we don't have to accept a check from someone else?

Obviously, you have to eat, and you need a roof over your head. And you have to have a source of income to pay for it. The problem arises when you realize that everyone else has an idea of what *you* should be doing with *your time.* In other words: if you don't choose a purpose, someone else probably has one for you.

I realized that it's not that hard to pay yourself to be who you are. As soon as I chose a purpose for myself, it became easy for me to see all the ways I could provide value to others while following it.

You have to choose your purpose. You have to choose the way you contribute value that is meaningful to others. You have to find a way to pay yourself for the value you share.

My Path Is Just One Path

Your path will be different. My path is just one path.

But you can use me and the other people I've featured in this book as an example to work out your own blueprint for making the transition to owning your own time.

Whatever you do, do not read this and look for excuses why this is not possible for you.

It is possible for you.

But you have to take action. Learning and reading is absolutely necessary, but only up to a point.

I want to help you make the change you want in your life. Please don't read this as entertainment. Do something with it.

Because if you don't implement, nothing will change. No action, no results.

The perfect time will not come. It never does.
Paths are made by walking.

Part 2

My Journey to Getting Paid to Be Me

A lot of people ask me how I've been able to achieve success online in the amount of time I have. While I'm very grateful to have acquired the success I've had, most of it has come through the *mindset* and strategies I've adopted, not the specific tactics.

With these strategies I've managed to build a blog with over 10,000 subscribers, create a full-time income online, and get a regular writing spot for a top 50 blog (ZenHabits.net).

What follows are the strategies I employed to get paid to be me, that had the greatest impact.

1. Creating a Clear, Remarkable Message

This is really where you have to start, and the core foundation that everything else is built upon. If you skimp and build a shallow foundation, everything else crumbles. So it's worth spending a good deal of time thinking about this, getting clarity about your message and what makes it remarkable.

A remarkable message that people can rally behind involves a few key ingredients:

• You are deeply passionate about it.

• It involves creating some kind of change, or an ideal that people are passionate about.

• It is remarkable, unique, and easily sharable with others. On Illuminated Mind, my message is: *To create a social movement based on authentic action; a revolution of people living on their own terms.*

This is my core message, and it's something others and myself are deeply passionate about. It's an idea that's remarkable so it's easy for other people to get excited about it and want to share it with others.

It took me a while to really get clear about this message, so don't feel like you have to figure this out overnight. It will take some time, but the best thing you can do is to plant the seeds right now for thinking about what your core message will be.

Ask yourself these questions:

• What makes me come alive?

• What kind of change do I want to see happen in the world?

• What type of people do I most resonate with? How can I speak to them?

• What are the connecting elements between me and the people I want to reach?

• How can I define what the goal of my work is in terms of a revolution or a social movement?

The biggest benefit about having an incredibly clear and remarkable message is that it allows the people that resonate with your cause to connect with you more easily.

Without that, you leave people guessing or trying to figure it out for themselves. You don't want people to have to decipher or decode the purpose of your website. It should be clear within 30 seconds what you're about and the core themes behind everything you do.

GO FURTHER: Check out "How to Start a Revolution":

http://www.illuminatedmind.net/2009/05/21/how-to-start-a-revolution/

and "Creating a Legacy Project":

http://chrisguillebeau.com/3x5/creating-a-legacy-project/

2. Tapping into Blogging and Social Media to Lead a Tribe of Passionate People

Targeting my message to the people that I most resonate with has been one of the biggest keys to my success. Before I did that, I tried to speak to everyone, and guess what happened? No one listened. When you direct your message to *your tribe,* on the other hand, you make them feel special. They instantly connect with you because they know you are speaking to them.

What Is a Tribe?

A tribe is a group of people who are insanely interested in a particular subject, topic, or thing. The more cult-like the following, the more powerful the tribe is.

Around every particular field, there will be a tribe that is highly interested in its study.

A few examples of tribes:

- Productivity geeks that constantly tweak their GTD systems.
- Hell's Angels.
- Football fans that paint their faces and go to every game.
- Sci-fi fans that practice "The Force" as a religion.
- Martial arts practitioners that painstakingly hone their skills. These are just a few examples of tribes, and chances are there will probably be a tribe surrounding your passion, whether it's knitting, interior design, or travel writing.

Your job is to connect with the people in your field that are insanely enthusiastic about what they do.

Before we get into how to connect with your tribe, let's answer a couple of questions:

1. *Why insanely interested?* The people that are insanely interested in your topic or passion are the most likely to spread your ideas. They are the ones that talk most about it; they are the ones looking for more information and better information. They want to know everything there is to know about it and be completely immersed in it. Naturally, if they like the

stuff you're doing, they will be likely to share it with others.

2. *Why do I want to connect with a tribe?* The answer to this question should be slightly obvious, because there is a common interest, but so many people do the opposite. They try to mass blanket their message to everyone and try to make connections with people in completely unrelated fields.

Think about it, who would you be more likely to want to build a relationship with and help? The person that has the same interests, values, and goals as you, or the person that you kind of like, but has none of the same interests, none of the same goals or ambitions?

Obviously, you would choose the first person. They're people that you want to have relationships with because like them, you respect them, and you have fun interacting with them. But not only are they fun to interact with, they're the people that will spread your message like wildfire.

So How Do You Find These People?

There are a potentially endless number of ways you can go about doing this, but the two that have been the most powerful for me are: *Blogging* and *Twitter*.

The Power of Blogging

Blogging naturally helps you connect with people in your tribe because you create a platform to continually share and expand on your message. Every time you write, you give your fans a chance to share your writing with other people in your tribe that they know.

There are tons of other reasons for having a blog which we won't get into here, but let's just say that blogging is one of the best ways to build relationships. You give away free content and free advice, and in return, build relationships. You can build that trust to offer a service like coaching or consulting, or you can use it to sell a product.

Blogging also allows you to demonstrate your expertise. Through means such as comments, subscribers, and fans, blogging also helps you establish "social proof." What that means is that once people see a history of your articles, comments, links, and the places you've been published, it establishes credibility.

Not only does blogging help you form relationships, it is one of the best ways to show someone that you know your stuff *before they buy from you.*

The side-benefit of blogging is that it helps you grow.

Every time you write an article, you're forced to gain a greater clarity and holistic understanding of the topic you're writing about. When you have to put what you're teaching into words, you're not only teaching others, you're teaching yourself.

Why Twitter Is Changing Everything

If you're in the "conversation," then you know that Twitter is completely changing the way we work and connect. It's easier than ever to connect with and find the people in your tribe by using Twitter.

Twitter is especially awesome because it breaks through the normal barriers of starting conversations. Since Twitter is created for the purpose of conversation, it eliminates the normal barriers to entry you would otherwise experience. I've had conversations with CEOs, thought leaders, best-selling authors, and A-List bloggers on Twitter that would have normally been nearly impossible to reach through conventional methods of communication.

Here are a few ways you can get started connecting with people in your tribe.

1. *Follow keywords.* Go to Twitter Pulse and type in the keywords you're looking for:

http://www.b2gmedia.com/twitterpulse.php

If you're a martial arts teacher looking to connect with other martial artists, an obvious keyword to track would be "martial arts." But you can also search for overlapping niches like fitness, self development, and health. Once you set this up, you'll be notified however often you want about tweets that contain your keywords. Now you can start joining the conversation with people that are passionate about your topic.

2. *Use a Twitter directory.* Directories like WeFollow.com and Twellow.com are becoming increasingly popular for listing yourself under certain topics and finding others with the same interests. Check out people's profiles you see talking about your topic, follow them and start conversations with them. Especially look for people with large numbers of followers. Try to connect with these people and study the way they use Twitter. Take advantage of these services for listing yourself and finding others, but know that this is only one possibility.

3. *Ask people to connect you.* This strategy is so simple and effective that I'm amazed more people don't use it. I regularly ask people on Twitter to connect me with other people they think I would like to follow or would find value from. I've found a lot of cool, helpful, and interesting people this way. It's incredibly easy to build relationships using this simple technique.

3. Ruthlessly Prioritizing Based on Highest Leverage Activities

If you want to create freedom and get paid to exist, you have to focus your energy and attention on tasks that are going to have the highest impact.

In case you were wondering . . . *checking email, site stats, and spending hours reading blog posts are* not *high leverage activities.*

In the age of the internet and the many communication tools we have available to us, it's easy to get distracted. We can spend hours or days doing things that keep us "busy," but at the end of the day, we don't have much to show for ourselves.

Two things have helped me solve this problem more than anything:

• Creating a list of my highest leverage tasks, and deliberately choosing what I'm going to work on each day.

• Being a part of an accountability/mastermind group. I believe that consciously and deliberately selecting your focus is the most powerful tool in creating the success you want.

Every project that I choose, I make sure that I evaluate whether or not it will have a high return on investment *before* I start on it. I meet with a group of entrepreneurs each week where we help each other choose our single highest leverage task for the week, and keep each other accountable for following through.

I highly recommend that you do these two things. If you can't find an existing accountability group, you can easily create one. Ask a few highly motivated people that you know to meet with you each week at a specific time. Each of you can hold each other accountable for doing the tasks you agree to. Do whatever it takes to make it easy for the other people. Offer to setup the meetings, send out the invites, and reminders.

Each week, take turns discussing each member's highest leverage task and what each person did the previous week. Make sure that the tasks you choose are demonstrable, or that you can offer some kind of proof that you did what you said you would. If you do just this one thing, I guarantee that your rate of following through will skyrocket.

4. Throwing Away ALL of the "Good Ideas"

When I first started writing, I would write a blog post about every idea that came to me. I would save all of my so-called "good ideas" and make sure that I never let any of them get away from me.

Now I've learned in order to be remarkable (worth talking about), I need to throw away the majority of my good ideas, and only keep the truly exceptional ones. I may have 30 or 40 ideas in my Google document titled "blog post ideas," but only two or three will actually be published.

When I decide to write about something, I ask myself one or more of these questions:

- Is this something that people would want to share with others?
- Are people desperate to know more about this? Or is everyone else already talking about it?
- If everyone else is talking about it, can I offer a unique or unconventional angle?
- Is anything about this contrarian, uncommon, or counterintuitive (my core writing themes)?

- Does it align with and build upon my core message?

If an idea doesn't meet this criteria, I simply do not write about it. I don't have time to work on *average stuff,* because I know that no one wants to read *average content.* (I certainly don't.)

I think of this mantra whenever I write: *If I'm not being remarkable, I'm contributing to the noise.*

I want people to be *insanely interested* in my writing. If *I* am not insanely interested in it, how can I expect other people to be?

GO FURTHER: Read "How to Create a Highly Viral Blog":

http://writetodone.com/2009/05/06/how-to-create-a-highly-viral-blog/

5. Build Meaningful, Win/Win Relationships (and Help Other People Get What They Want)

There is no way I could have achieved the success I have today without all the help and support I have received along the way.

This support has come from people that have much more experience and success than me ("big people"), those that are at or around my level, and those just starting out. All of them are important in building your brand and creating a following.

Here's what you need to remember: No one is "too big" for you to build a relationship with, and no one is "too little," either.

When building relationships with others here are the keys:

- You have some type of overlapping audience and follower-base.
- You have similar interests, goals, and directions.
- You are both highly passionate about and motivated toward long-term success.
- You are able to help them get what they want.

I've also built relationships with people that others probably thought were "too inexperienced." But I saw what they didn't see: they were highly motivated, passionate, and willing to work hard. I knew that they would gain influence quickly and I could see that they were dedicated and not going to "disappear" tomorrow when they didn't achieve overnight success.

I knew that while these people might not be influential now, it was just a matter of time before they became big stars. It makes sense to help these people, because they will remember it. You can try to help a lot of big names, but more often than not, you will be seen as just another person vying for their attention.

To avoid that, the best thing way to connect with busy, successful people is to:

- Respect their time. Know what you want to say and make sure you say it clearly and succinctly.
- Bypass clogged communication channels. Email and Facebook are probably the most clogged channels. Try connecting in a different way, maybe on

Twitter first, then build the intimacy of the conversation to Skype, phone, or an in-person meetup.

- If you have mutual connections, ask for an introduction.
- Try to find a backdoor or uncommon shared interest. I receive a lot of communications every day through email and Twitter, and a lot of them I don't pay much attention to because I don't resonate with that person. But if I knew if they had an uncommon shared interest with me, say, raw food-ism or Jeet Kune Do, then I would be more likely to want to connect with that person.
- Offer some kind of value to that person, and have a genuine desire for connecting. Don't just seek relationships because you want to get something from someone.

Ultimately, you should seek to connect and build relationships with people that are around your level or higher, so you know you will be encouraged to grow. But don't underestimate rising stars either, and those that are just starting out on their path. They will often turn out to become your biggest fans and greatest support.

GO FURTHER: Read "How to Make Deals with Big Shots in Less Than Ten Minutes," by Laura Roeder:

http://www.problogger.net/archives/2009/01/19/how-to-make-deals-with-bigshots-in-less-than-10-minutes/

6. Do What I Want While Giving People What They Want

This is really what it all comes down to, and is pretty much where everything else comes together. If you can't do what you want, while providing value to others, you can't make a profit and you can't actually get paid to do what you love.

So in order to get paid to exist, you have to do something you absolutely love and find a way to provide value to others while you're doing it.

That might mean delivering that value in the form of:

- An ebook.
- Membership site or continuity program.
- Video training.
- Live workshops.
- Teleseminars.
- A physical product.
- Consulting.
- Coaching.

These are just a few possibilities, but this is the *way you deliver the value,* not the actual value you deliver.

So you ultimately need to figure out what people desperately want or need.

This is a combination of what you're interested in, and what your fans are desperately seeking. In other words, it's about identifying a *gap*. You want to find those gaps and fill them.

There might be a gap in information, education, or advice. There might be a gap in the way a product is delivered. Or there might be a gap because there is already a product, but it's not being marketed in a way that speaks to your audience. If you can do a better job speaking to your audience and building trust, you will consistently win their favor.

How Do You Know What Your Followers Want?

Here are a few suggestions for getting to know what your followers want (instead of trying to read their minds):

• Create a survey with open-ended questions like "What's your biggest question about [your topic]?" and "What your biggest frustration about [your topic]?"

• If you have an idea for a product, write about the topic on your blog first and gauge the reaction. If you don't have a big following, try borrowing someone else's blog (guest posting) or poll a popular forum or community.

• Ask how people feel about your idea on Twitter, Facebook, or your social media outlet of choice. Pay attention the response you get.

It's really that simple. Ask people what they want, and then give it to them.

But most people do the perfect opposite. They try to "read their customer's mind" and decide what the customer wants because they're supposed to be the "expert."

This is exactly what you don't want to do. Even if you think you know exactly what your customer needs (and you may be right), ask them anyway. Then you'll know for sure, and you'll know that you've made the sale *before* you've made the product.

That's what I (unknowingly) did before I started writing my ebook *Reclaim Your Dreams—An Uncommon Guide to Living on Your Own Terms:*

http://illuminatedmind.net/reclaim-your-dreams

I had been wanting to write an ebook to sell on my blog for a long time. So when I came up with the idea about reclaiming your dreams, I thought it would be something a lot of people would be interested in. But before I wrote it, I wanted to make sure the interest was there, so I decided to write a series on living your dreams first. The series was a huge success, especially the post "The Number One Dream Killer: Doing What Works":

http://www.illuminatedmind.net/2008/10/22/the-number-one-dream-killer-doing-what-works/

Once I noticed that there was an interest, I decide to poll my readers. I asked them: "What's the biggest obstacle for you in making your dreams a reality?" After receiving nearly a hundred responses I decided that there was *definitely* an interest. And it also seemed like there was a huge demand (gap) that wasn't being met.

I tested the demand before I wrote the ebook, and it paid off. *Reclaim Your Dreams* continues to be a strong seller and the revenue from it still makes up over a third of my income.

I actually did this half on accident. I didn't know about creating surveys and asking targeted open-ended questions. I was lucky to at least have the intuition to notice that I got a good response and that creating an ebook about this was a good idea.

Now imagine what you can do knowing this stuff *before you start*.

Hindsight Is 20/20—the Mistakes and Lessons I Learned Along the Way

When I first started my blog, I made the mistake of trying to speak to *everyone*. I hadn't written much in the past, so I wasn't sure of my voice. Luckily, I realized that in order for me to set myself apart, I would have to stop trying to be everything to everyone and home in on the people that most resonated with my message.

The more I wrote and the more encouragement I got, the more I felt empowered to be brazen in my writing and "walk the edges."

If I had to do it all over again, I would have trusted myself to speak in my own voice in the beginning, instead of trying to copy others and write for everyone.

The Social Media Black Hole

The other hard lesson I learned was to not waste my time with social media sites like Digg and Stumbleupon. I tried to joining social networking groups where people would help each other with votes, and I also spent a lot of time trying to befriend and gain favor from the "power users." All of this ended up being a huge waste of time.

Even if I hit the front page of Digg (which I did once) or went popular on StumbleUpon or some other social voting site, the quality of traffic was often very poor. The bounce rate was huge (how many people leave your site without clicking anywhere else); somewhere around 80%, when I was targeting these sites.

The main lesson I learned was not to pay too much attention to traffic and stats. You can have a lot of page views, Twitter followers, or RSS subscribers and it could not mean much. If they don't *care* much about the stuff you're doing and are just another bullet point in their feed reader. You have no leverage.

It's much better to have a tighter community that is deeply passionate, than a huge community that is completely passive.

Now I care much more about the impact that I'm making, rather than the constantly fluctuating stats.

My Big, Fat, Embarrassing Mistake: the One 99% of Bloggers Make and the Reason They Never Quit Their Jobs

When I first started my blog, I wanted to become a "problogger." I thought I could start a blog, post every day and within a few months have thousands of subscribers, make a million dollars a month from AdSense and happily quit my day job.

Well, that ~~failed miserably~~ didn't really work.

When most people start blogging with the ambition of turning it into a means of income (so they can quit their job) they have the wrong mindset.

Here's the typical "green blogger" strategy:

"If only I can get enough subscribers, enough traffic and enough readers, then I can find a way to turn that traffic into an income."

This strategy is so backwards to making money, it rarely ever works. With this frame of mind, the goal is to get an enormous amount of subscribers (perhaps 50,000), and try to convert that popularity into making money.

What I call this person is *The Blogger Who Attempts to Monetize Traffic.*

This is not the person that you want to be if you ever want to quit your day job and get paid to exist.

The person you want to be is *The Business Owner Who Blogs to Build Relationships, Gives Value, and Qualifies Potential Buyers.*

You will have other reasons for blogging of course. It helps you learn, clarify your thoughts, and grow as a person. It allows you to create community and purpose.

Not to mention, blogging is a lot of fun; for me at least.

Keeping Perspective

Those are all wonderful things, but if you don't see yourself as a business owner first, and a blogger second, you will have a hard time making money online.

This was the fatal mistake I made when I first started blogging. Unfortunately for me, and most others, blogging and Google AdSense is *not* a business model.

So get your business straight. Work on your marketing, optimizing, creating useful products, building relationships and time management. Then use blogging as a tool to help you build credibility, gain trust and get exposure.

Business owner first, blogger second.

It's important to note here that these were the biggest keys in my own success. While I think most of these ideas are sound principles anyone can apply, your mileage may vary.

But please, don't look at me and think "Okay, well that's all good and fine for him. He's different. But that could never happen for me."

I am just like you. I have the same fears. I had the same dissatisfaction with the status quo, and I started at the same place as everyone else: the beginning.

The thing is, we have a tendency to overestimate what others are capable of, and underestimate ourselves.

But it's not just that.

What we see at first glance is the massive success. We see the people who have done what we only dream of, at the top of the mountain. What we don't see is the journey that they took to get there. We don't see all the small steps; one foot in front of the other, every day for months or years.

Every day I wake up with a sense of gratitude and thankfulness that I am able to do what I do for a living. Sometimes I think I'm lucky, but I remember all the days that I often worked on my blog during dinner, on the weekends and while others were sleeping.

I remember I would get frustrated looking at the people I admired and wanted to emulate. I saw their massive success and wondered why I couldn't be so lucky. But what I forgot to see was each step they took along the way.

So if you think that it will take a lot of work, you're right. If you think you might have some ideas that fail, you're right. But if you think you can keep putting one foot in front of the other a thousand times and not get *anywhere,* you're wrong.

There's an old Chinese saying that says "The man

who can rise before dawn 360 days a year, never fails to make his family rich."

If you keep *showing up* it will be inevitable that you will succeed.

Part 3

Zero-Hour Case Studies

Since I began my online entrepreneurial journey, I've had the pleasure of meeting several renegades who are really living the stuff that I'm talking about.

These strategies can actually be done in the real world, and actually work when they're practiced. I know they do because I've seen it, over and over. Not only do they work, but they're massively more effective than the alternative (working at a job you hate).

Imagine how much easier it would be to totally kick ass at something you *love doing*. Imagine how much more effortless it would be to shake the earth with your message, when you actually *care* about that message.

That's what these people I'm about to introduce you to are doing. They are rocking the entrepreneurial world.

They're doing stuff they are insanely passionate about.

They are helping others and creating change.

More than anything, they are forces to be reckoned with because they cannot be stopped. How can you stop someone that loves what they do?

You can't.

Here's what they had to say.

Danielle Laporte / whitehottruth.com

One of the things I've noticed about getting paid to exist is that it's often hard to answer the question "What do you do?" Danielle is a perfect example of that.

Professionally, she writes and inspires on her trailblazing blog. She jams with entrepreneurs on how to rock their careers, and speaks to audiences about liberating their authentic power. She does many things, but most importantly, she's about making a difference while taking passionate, authentic action.

ON THE IMPORTANCE OF AUTHENTICITY

"Authenticity is magnetic. It's that simple. Everyone craves genuine connection. It's human nature. But it's also human nature to want to fit in. So we game-play. When you can stay anchored to your original self and package it in a way that your key audience can hear you, then that's clarity—and not a whole lot of people have the courage to do that. But that directness creates connection and interest from others, and that usually leads to earning cash or prosperity in some form."

DANIELLE'S TIPS FOR ROCKING YOUR PERSONAL BRAND

1. Speak in first person. For God's sake, everyone knows that you wrote your own bio on your site. Just speak as you are. One on one. Go direct. Your audience wants to hear you, not your copywriter or your most uptight version of you.

2. Practice elegance. One of my favorite definitions of elegance is from Antoine de Saint-Exupéry, the author of *The Little Prince,* who said that "elegance is when there is nothing left to add, and nothing left to take away." So you can still be punk or eccentric or warrior, and be elegant in terms of your presentation. Simple and honest.

3. Be truly useful. The purpose of branding is commerce, which means you're exchanging your stuff for someone else's form of stuff. Don't wank. Before you press send, or pick up the phone, or put your widget out into the world, you need to feel in your bones that you're doing something that's going to improve things in some modest way. All good, sustainable things come from that pure intention.

Chris Guillebeau / artofnonconformity.com

Chris is a writer, entrepreneur, and world traveler. Through his website he promotes changing the world

(World Domination, as he calls it) through living remarkably, and world travel.

This quote encapsulates Chris's message well:

"Once in a while it really hits people that they don't have to experience the world in the way they have been told to."—Alan Keightley

Why He Thinks the World Needs People to Do What They Love for a Living

"If consensus is overrated, I think balance is too. I have no interest in living a balanced life. I want a life of adventure, and I know that many of the people who read this will identify with similar ideas. I have little patience for anyone who tries to prevent someone else from doing what they are passionate about. Get out there, do great stuff, and don't worry too much about anyone who doesn't like it."

If He Had to Start All Over

"The business side of what I do developed quite organically. It's fairly strategic now in the sense that I know where I'm going—but I guess if anything I would have started sooner. The best time to start anything is usually now—we can't change the past, and the future is only partly in our hands."

Chris's tips for social media success:

1. Oscar Wilde put it best: *"Be yourself, because everyone else is already taken."*

2. That said, not every aspect of who you are or what you do is interesting to other people. The goal is to find the convergence between what you love and what other people are interested in.

3. Consensus is overrated! Stand out somehow.

Glen Allsopp / pluginid.com

Glenn is a personal development writer and online entrepreneur. He has gained a surprisingly large audience on his blog PluginID in relatively little time with his always interesting and personal articles.

How Being Remarkable Has Played into His Success

"At all times I try to follow my gut instinct and while that often takes me down unknown territory, it also means everything I do is both helping people due to my raw honesty and unique because I'm going by my own intuition. I think that has helped my success because people can really relate to whatever I put out there."

How Getting Paid to Be Who He Is Has Changed His Life

"The main benefit I always preach is that my work revolves around my life, not my life around work. I like to think of my online projects as not who I am and what I do, but like an amplification of what I do offline in terms of the audience that gets to see it."

The Importance of Being Authentic

"Be Real. I say this all the time, but that's because it is so important. If you can't follow this simple step, good luck in trying to leverage the social web. This seems obvious, but it's hard for a lot of people. They might put on a corporate front, go by a nickname or just talk to you in some generic tone."

On Giving Your Fans What They Want

"Don't shout, listen. I regularly see small business owners, new bloggers and even corporate companies try to push their message out onto people.

You can't just go into a platform like Twitter, Facebook or Digg and try to "force" your messages on people.

You have to listen and interact with these people. Make and sustain connections if you want to leverage any of these communities. And don't see it as some devious trick to get more of what you want; I mean create real connections that stick."

Nathalie Lussier / rawfoodswitch.com

Nathalie is someone that you don't meet and easily forget. Her style and attitude makes her someone you easily connect with.

Nathalie helps people overcome their fears of "raw food magick" so they can live a healthy and empowered life.

Being an (aspiring) raw foodist myself, I was impressed by the way Nathalie found a way to market herself as a coach and teacher. Raw living is typically seen as something "weird" or "extreme" and Nathalie has done a great job of dispelling a lot of those myths.

WHAT MAKES HER AMAZING

"I don't push people to go 100% raw, and I mix modern day science with traditional systems of healing. Plus, I call myself The Raw Foods Witch. I give people permission to be where they are when they first start learning about raw food. It makes it more accessible, and also more fun, which is what has helped me spread my message. In turn, the mix of modern and traditional has helped me better serve my clients."

IF SHE HAD TO START ALL OVER

"I would have built relationships with people in my industry before starting my business. The funniest part is that I had all of the connections, I just wasn't nurturing them. That meant that I just showed up out of the blue as a "newbie" on the raw food scene, even though I had been around (but lurking) for over three years."

HOW GETTING PAID TO BE WHO SHE IS HAS CHANGED HER LIFE

"It has done tremendous things for my confidence, my relationships, and my creativity. I've always been a creative person, but now that I'm allowed and even expected to bring my creativity to everything I do, I'm really thriving. Every day is a fun new experience, and I love the constant feedback loop from idea-creation-reply between me and my readers/clients."

Cody Mckibben / thrillingheroics.com

Digital nomad, world traveler, web technology consultant, and activist make up the life of Cody McKibben. His passion is helping people make a difference in the world.

Through his business Cody helps to create change by devoting a portion of his time and profits to the local charity and volunteer organization in Bangkok—In Search of Sanuk:

http://www.insearchofsanuk.com/

WHY HE THINKS THE WORLD NEEDS PEOPLE TO DO WHAT THEY LOVE FOR A LIVING

"People who love what they do simply do it better than people who are "just doing their job"! I don't know yet if a world where everyone truly loves their work is possible, but I know that the individuals who make the biggest impact in the world and move society towards positive social change definitely tend to enjoy their work so much that they work 60–80 hour weeks. It doesn't feel like work for them!"

IF HE HAD TO START ALL OVER

"I find that there are things you are good at, things that you enjoy doing, and things that you can get paid for. There is a small area where they overlap, and that is where your business will be most successful. To be honest, I got my start doing things I was good at and could get paid for but that I wasn't that excited by. So it can be a struggle to reposition yourself and focus more on the things you enjoy. Try to remain focused on the things that you really enjoy and are passionate about from the very beginning and you'll be on the path to getting paid to be you!"

ON EMPOWERING YOUR TRIBE

"Build your community wisely. Use tools like Twitter and Facebook to connect with like-minded people. Answer comments and emails from your website. Be helpful, answer questions (LinkedIn Answers, Twitter search, and Yahoo Answers are good for this). Address complaints and misunderstandings amicably. Find and empower the biggest influencers in your community—let your followers shine!—and continually, graciously thank and reward your True Fans!"

Charlie Gilkey / productiveflourishing.com

Charlie does something beautiful for people that is hard to describe. To attempt to put in words, he helps creative people do their thing instead of just thinking about it, but it's actually much cooler than that.

What makes Charlie especially unique is that because of his broad experience, he's really good at using both sides of his brain: creative and logical. He uses this gift to help people gain creative clarity, and *actually figure out what to do with it.*

WHAT MAKES HIM REMARKABLE

"There are plenty of people who are insanely creative or incredibly logical, but it's apparently hard to find people who are both who can also help others. Being able to riff with ideas for a half-hour and then flip a switch and talk about what to do with them, all in a way that makes it seem approachable and doable, is what helps me help my people get the momentum going with meaningful action."

HOW GETTING PAID TO BE WHO HE IS HAS CHANGED HIS LIFE

"In some ways, most of the struggles of trying to be who others wanted me to be has subsided. The more I lean into who I am and what I do, the easier life becomes. But perhaps the most salient thing to me, right now, is that happiness isn't something that comes after my work; it comes during it."

Charlie's Tips for Rocking Social Media

1. Remember that no matter how you do it, you're talking to people.

2. Finding your voice is more important than figuring out the tricks.

3. It's easier to get people's attention if *what you're doing* does the talking.

Part 4

Your Paid-to-Exist Secret Weapon

Besides learning from my story about how I got paid to be me, I wanted to see if I could help you find a way to figure out how *you* can get paid to exist. There are a lot of elements toward creating this lifestyle, but I think the most important is your "secret weapon."

In order to truly get paid to be *who you are,* you must be excited about the *value* you are contributing to others.

This is the hub of the wheel that all of the other spokes stem from. Without this part, nothing really matters.

So this is the most important thing you can work on. If you only get one thing out of reading this, this is what I'd like to help you with most.

Getting paid to exist is about eliminating the lines between "work" and "life." It's about demolishing the disconnect between *the value you create for others* on the one hand, and *the passion and natural talents you have* on the other.

If you're creating brake parts for a living (something other people value), but you don't (1) give a hoot about brake parts (no passion) and (2) are not good at creating brake parts (no natural talent), there is a major disconnect. Not only are you not good at it, but you could care less about it. It's simply doing something to pay the bills. You're in survival mode, not living mode.

It's also important to note that if you love collecting stamps, but (1) no one else cares (no value to others) and (2) you really suck at it (no natural strengths), then there is not a very good potential that you'll get paid to do it.

Getting paid to exist is about eliminating those disconnects.

You want to do what you love, are naturally good at, and provide others with massive value at the same time.

It should be pretty obvious by now that your "paid to exist secret weapon" has three main elements:

1. It has the potential to provide others with value they are willing to pay for.

2. It leverages some type of natural talent or strength you've had since birth.

3. You love to do it, and your passion for it is sustainable (you won't get tired of it in three weeks).

These three components are what comprises your secret weapon.

To use myself as a personal example:

How I get paid to exist, or "what I do," is teach self-development that speaks to unconventional people, helps them wake up excited about their lives, live authentically, and on their own terms.

Let's take a look at how this breaks down:

1. *Does it provide value to others?* Yes. People are highly interested in living on their own terms and are willing to pay someone to help guide them. I provide this value exchange in the form of free articles, paid and free ebooks, and paid life coaching. I build trust by building a relationship of intimacy from free articles, to increasingly higher exchanges of value.

2. *Does it leverage some type of natural talent or strength I've had since birth?* Yes. I've always had a curious, questioning spirit. I've always had a natural ability to look at things holistically and get to the root of the issue. I use this unique strength to see the limiting beliefs and patterns in others. By easily identifying the root cause of someone's self- defeating patterns, I am able to find the best way to solve the problem at a core level.

3. *Do I love to do it and is my passion sustainable?* Yes, I absolutely love problem-solving, exploring different ways of looking at life, and helping others.

By helping others with their own self-development, I naturally help myself as well. It's a win/win. This is not something I'd get bored or tired of easily, because self-development encompasses so many opportunities for learning and going deeper. In short, *there is always another level I can aspire to reach.*

Can you see why finding an intersection like this is so important? This overlap is what makes your means of supporting yourself so natural that it doesn't feel like work. It may take effort, but it is not a chore you dread, or a grim duty.

When I'm working in my business, I never feel like I have to force myself to be productive. I am naturally drawn to it, because teaching and learning is just something that I love doing. Sometimes I am so enthralled with the work that I'm doing that I have to consciously pull myself away from it so I don't burn out. *That* is the way work should be.

I've looked at countless others who are rocking their careers and getting paid to be who they are, and Value, Passion and Strengths are the three main elements that show up in all of them. There are some other important aspects of getting paid to exist that you can leverage, as well. But those three things make up the trunk of your tree. The rest are branches.

Now that you have a clear understanding of the elements to your "secret weapon," let's get into the logistics of how you'll actually figure this out for yourself.

How to Find Your Secret Weapon

This is actually a very easy process; much easier than most people make it. When I talk about these three elements and finding an intersection, it can be easy to feel overwhelmed at the daunting task of finding this "sweet spot." We're going to avoid this overwhelming feeling by reverse engineering the process, and isolating to one area at a time in a progressive way.

Step One: Ask Yourself, "What Am I Passionate About That I Could Do for a Living?"

You would be amazed at how many people want to do what they love for a living, but they never take the time to ask themselves this question. Maybe you've given this some thought, or maybe you haven't. Either way, you need to take the time to ask yourself this question.

Maybe you're afraid that you're not passionate about anything. Well, perhaps this is only true because you've never given yourself *permission* to be passionate. So give yourself permission and ask "What am I passionate about that I could do for a living?"

Come up with at least 20 answers to this question, be ridiculous if you need to. (You have my permission.)

Try to think in these terms: "How can I do something that deeply fulfills and excites me, while providing value and making a difference to others?"

EXERCISE: Read the free report "7 Keys to Discovering Your Passion" by signing up for my newsletter *The* Un*stream:*

http://www.illuminatedmind.net/the-unstream/

Answer and go through all of the exercises within.

STEP TWO: ASK YOURSELF, "OF THESE 20 POSSIBILITIES, WHICH OF THEM COULD UTILIZE UNIQUE PERSONAL STRENGTHS THAT I'VE HAD SINCE BIRTH?"

This is about figuring out where your love and your natural abilities collide. The key here is to focus on core strengths; areas where you excel far beyond the capabilities others normally possess.

Some examples of these core strengths might be:

- Communication.
- Cultivating Relationships.
- Problem Solving.
- Design.
- Teaching.
- Simplifying.
- Empathy.
- Organization.
- Visualizing.
- Systemic Thinking.
- Inspiring Others.
- Leading Others.

These are just a few examples, and obviously many of these qualities and traits can be learned and developed. But there are some of these things that you are *naturally* gifted at doing. I am naturally gifted at thinking holistically and philosophically. Because of that, it's easy for me to see the root of people's problems and help them solve them.

Why We Want Strength/Passion Intersections We could just as easily choose something we're not naturally gifted at and train it to a level of competency.

But that is not what we want to do here. We want to find a way to leverage our natural strengths to magnify our passion. By doing this, two things happen:

1. *We lessen the gap of time between finding our secret weapon, and getting paid to use it.* In other words, it's easier for us to move swiftly from the point of ground zero and no customer base, to profitability. Since we're already good at it, we don't have to waste precious time trying to hone or learn new skills. By working from your strengths—rather than trying to improve your weaknesses—you'll be a hundred times more effective.

2. *You utilize your competitive edge.* If you're naturally gifted at something, and other people are struggling to just get *close* to your skill level, you are going to have a huge advantage. You'll easily excel while others are just trying to be competent.

EXERCISE: Sometimes it's difficult for us to see what we're good at because we're so good at it, and it's so natural that it's not obvious to us. It can be helpful in this situation to ask someone else what we're good at.

So, pick three people to interview about your personal strengths and natural talents:

1. A parent, sibling or close relative,
2. A peer or someone you've worked with, or
3. A partner or friend.

Look at the common themes in their responses.

STEP THREE: ASK YOURSELF "HOW WILL I DO [YOUR IDEA] IN A WAY THAT PROVIDES VALUE TO OTHERS?"

This is arguable the most important part of the process.

Once you've discovered your greatest passion/strength intersections, now you need to determine if and how you can do provide value by doing it.

To determine the value of your possible endeavor, think about these questions:

- What benefits will me doing this provide others?
- How will those benefits be delivered? (Physical product, ebook, consulting, coaching, webinar, etc.)
- Is there a potential desperate or urgent need for what I'm offering? This is where you really determine if your idea has any potential in allowing you to get paid to exist.

If you find this value part challenging, try looking at it from the angle of "how will I contribute to others," rather than "how will I get people to give me their money." Money is simply an abstraction. *Value,* on the other hand, is what is really being exchanged.

EXERCISE: Define the three tangible benefits your customer will gain through interacting with you. Where are they now, and where will they be once they've worked with you, or used your product?

Okay, so those are the three steps:

1. Finding your passion;
2. Finding your strengths; and
3. Finding your value or finding your market.

I realize that this is going to be *the most challenging thing* for you on the path to getting paid to exist. After you come up with your list of ideas and intersections, it will be hard not to over-analyze and second guess whether or not you have a long-term potential with your ideas.

Because of that, I've created a special test called the Passion + Profits Test:

http://paidtoexist.net/test/

Once you have your list of ideas that meet the three criteria of passion, innate strength, and massive value to others, go through the test.

There is a video included in the test that explains each question and how it applies to you. After you watch the video and come up with your ideas, you'll rate each question on a scale of 1–5. When you finish, you'll receive an average score of how you rated each answer.

Complete the test with as many ideas you need until you come up with one that has a 4–5 average score.

Avoiding the Two Major Pitfalls

While I think I've covered all the bases here, there are, however, two major pitfalls that you should be aware of when turning your passion into a source of income.

1. Your beliefs. Do you believe that you don't deserve to do what you love for a living? Do you believe that work *must* be a chore? If so, you will never feel comfortable getting paid to exist. And even if you do figure out what you're passionate about, you will sabotage yourself before you allow it to become your main source of income. Above all, work on your belief that doing what you love for a living is your birthright.

Once you start questioning your beliefs about what you think is and is not possible, you will start getting a huge internal pushback. This is completely normal. You're basically revolting against a mental framework you've lived around for years or decades. But keep your mind open.

When you come up against a belief that you think is impossible—say, for instance, "I could never teach skydiving for a living"—*test it*. Is it really true that it's not possible? What is the market demand? How long does it take? What's the barrier to entry? Could I market myself in a different way than others that would allow me to sneak in a back door?

Ask yourself those questions, then *test your belief.* Is it fact, or myth? Assumption or truth?

2. The desire to be monogamous. It's also important to note that when getting paid to exist, you don't have to be monogamous. You may not just have "one true love" as a passion. You might have many.

In this case, you have a choice. Choosing one passion to be your source of income doesn't mean that you have to martyr the others. And sometimes choosing not to pursue your true love as a source of income can keep it sacred. I'll give you a personal example.

Since a young age, I have always loved playing music. I started playing Trombone in sixth grade, studied voice in junior high, and picked up guitar in high school. Then I finally found my true love: the djembe.

For a long time, I wanted to play music professionally. I considered doing this as something I loved, but every time I thought of playing music for a living, it made me cringe. I couldn't imagine feeling like I *must create* in order to pay the bills. I decided that while it would be cool to play music for a living, have fame and fortune and all of that, it wasn't something I wanted to pursue. *I just didn't think my love for music could take the stress of doing it as a means of income.*

That's when I got into blogging and writing on personal development. I decided that I would rather keep my music sacred and make my means of financial independence teaching personal development.

This is an perfect fit for me. I still enjoy playing music on the side and jamming with my friends, but I don't aspire to do it to pay the bills.

This may or may not be the same for you. You may have more grit than me and are more able to endure the stress that seeking an income from producing personal art can create. If so, more power to you.

Whatever you decide, realize that you can choose to pursue whatever passion you like.

Putting It All Together

Okay, by now you should have figured out what you're going to do to get paid to exist.

- You should know that it is something you're intrinsically good it.
- It should be something that sets your heart on fire and keeps you up at night.
- And lastly, it's something other people find immensely valuable. In other words, this is your contribution to the world.

Congratulations! You are 99% further along in life than many people will ever be.

You're well on your way to creating a Zero Hour Workweek.

Part 5

The World Needs You to Do What You Love

This may seem kind of crazy, but I think the world actually *needs you* to get paid to do what you love.

After all, don't you think you'll have a greater impact on the collective happiness of the planet if you're actually excited about the work you're doing? (If you can even call it work anymore.)

See, the really cool thing about doing what you love is that it's easier to be amazing at what you're doing. It's easy to excel. It's easy to connect. And it's easy to lead and build a following when you're excited about what you do for a living.

The other awesome side effect is that you'll be inspiring other people to do the same. The more people that break away and reject the idea that work must be a chore, the more we give everyone else the silent permission to do the same.

I believe it's our personal responsibility to help shift the paradigm of work to a new definition.

One of meaning, contribution, sacredness, and enjoyment.

So, I don't think what we're really looking for is a four hour work week, automated income, or early retirement. Those things might be nice, but they still don't get to the point.

That's because they reinforce the idea that we need to escape from work, when all work really is is the exchange of value with others. We obviously need to contribute and provide others with value to get paid, and to live, but that's only part of it. Deep down, we all desperately want to contribute. We want to participate. We want to help. We want to be heard. We want to be involved, immersed, and we want to share with others.

But we want to do it in a way that allows us to share our gifts, work on exciting things with people we like, and make a difference in the world.

That is the way all value should be exchanged. That is what it means to get paid to be who you are.

We don't really want to escape work or contribution. We just want to give the kind of value that we *want* to give. We want to decide the way we contribute. We want to work toward our own goals of contribution, instead of someone else's. But most of all, we want to contribute to something we believe in, are passionate about, and excited about.

You'll Probably Have to Create It

There may be the perfect job out there that aligns with your passions, utilizes your unique strengths, is remarkable, and pays you well to do it.

And you might even be able to find that amazing company where you love the people you work for and you love the people you work with. You might even find a place where they let you choose the projects you work on, and when you work on them.

The truth is, that elusive job may or may not exist. *But you can create it.*

After all, when you create it, you put the power back in your hands.

So go. Start now.

We need your gifts. We need you to be excited. We need you to love the work you do, and the people you work with.

Most of all, we need your contribution.

What's Next?

Take the Passion + Profits Test:
http://paidtoexist.net/test/

I know a lot of people never get the courage to follow their dreams, or quit their jobs because they're afraid of failing.

They're afraid they'll waste a lot of time and their idea won't be any good. They're afraid that no one will want to pay them to do what they love.

I got tired of seeing this, so I created a test to help people gain confidence in their idea before they start.

The Passion + Profits Test will help you figure out where your passions, strengths and values intersect.

I've worked with a lot of people that come to me for help on finding this unique "sweet spot."

If you want to get paid to do what you love, this test is a good a way to start.

Share

If you got something out of this book, I would really appreciate it if you could share it with a friend. I'd like to see as many people as possible be able to get paid to do what they love for a living, and I think you'd agree that the world would be a better place if more of us did.

How you can help:

• Email this link to a friend:

http://www.illuminatedmind.net/2009/09/08/the-zero-hour-workweek/

Send it to someone you think would benefit from it.

• Tweet about it:

http://budurl.com/0HWW

Click the "tweet this" button at the bottom of the page.

• Link to it:

http://www.illuminatedmind.net/2009/09/08/the-zero-hour-workweek/

The absolute coolest think you could do would be to link to or review this ebook on your blog.

Acknowledgments

A lot of people have helped along the way to making Illuminated Mind a success.

Thank you . . .

Charlie Gilkey for being a great friend, coach, and an awesome person.

Leo Babauta for taking the chance on me and giving me the opportunity to speak to the readers of Zen Habits, and putting up with my crazy ideas.

Clay and Laura for being amazing friends and mentors.

My wife, Ev'Yan, for believing in my crazy ideas and being my biggest fan.

And most importantly, thank you to all of my readers, everyone who has linked to me, retweeted my articles, or told your friends about them.

You are awesome. Thank you for allowing me to be a part of such an amazing community.

I seriously can't believe I get paid to do this stuff.

www.ingramcontent.com/pod-product-compliance
Lightning Source LLC
Chambersburg PA
CBHW061247040426
42444CB00010B/2277